Making~sense~out~of~suffering Therapy

Making~sense~out~of~suffering Therapy

written by
Jack Wintz, O.S.F

illustrated by
R.W. Alley

ONE
CARING
PLACE

Abbey Press

Text © 1996 by Jack Wintz, O.S.F.
Illustrations © 1996 by St. Meinrad Archabbey
Published by One Caring Place
Abbey Press
St. Meinrad, Indiana 47577

Library of Congress Catalog Number
96-85000

ISBN 0-87029-296-X

Printed in the United States of America

Foreword

The question of suffering has long confounded humans. But when suffering—concretely, specifically—enters your life, it becomes more than a question to engage the mind. It is, instead, an experience that confronts and overwhelms you emotionally, physically, and spiritually.

There are no easy checklists for coping with suffering; there's no quick solution for ending your turmoil and confusion and pain. *Making-sense-out-of-suffering Therapy* won't promise you any of that. But it will walk with you as you struggle with this difficult and inevitable reality. And it will offer insights, wisdom, inspiration that can move you to deeper understanding.

We can't choose whether we'll suffer. Being human means that we will. We live, after all, in an incomplete universe where we're free to make flawed choices. But we can choose how we respond to suffering. And it's out of our response—a loving, profound, God-centered response—that meaning comes.

Just as gold is purified by fire, so can the human heart be purified by suffering. *Making-sense-out-of-suffering Therapy* points the way to transformation, so that having responded generously to the trials of life, your heart may glow with new radiance.

1.

Wounds are a part of life, but the God who heals wounds is a much deeper reality. Seek the deeper reality; seek God—the Doctor of your soul.

2.

Be open to your suffering and hurt. Your human frailty can be the gate through which the God of love is found.

3.

Let your tears flow forth honestly within your own soul, with trusted persons, and before God. Releasing your tears opens the window to healing.

4.

Stay in touch with all the turmoil in your heart: anxiety, denial, fear, anger, sudden shifts between hope and despair. Your true feelings are the clearest channels you have for dialoguing with God and other loving friends.

5.

Keep close to the people you love and count on for support. Their compassionate presence and hugs are an important source of comfort and faith.

6.

Suffering makes no sense in itself, but trusting God under all circumstances leads, in time, to profound meaning. So take God's hand and walk bravely forward.

7.

When tragedy strikes, it's
normal to assault heaven
with a list of painful whys.
Why suffering? Why is this
happening to me? Why now?
Why do innocent people suffer?
Allow yourself to ask the
questions.

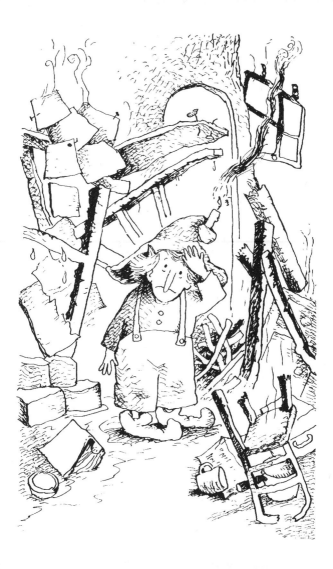

8.

When wrestling with the <u>why</u> of suffering doesn't solve its riddle, try focusing on the <u>Who</u>—the Compassionate Healer and Source of Wisdom who accompanies you through the dark valley.

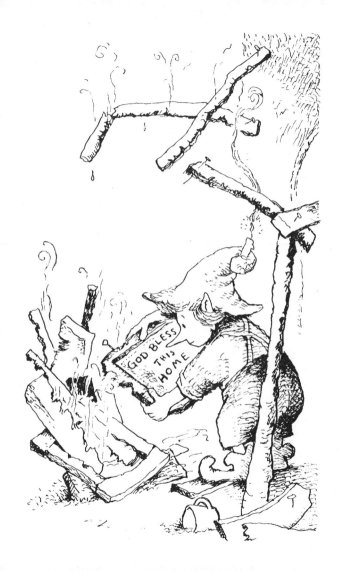

GOD BLESS THIS HOME

9.

You may also struggle with <u>what</u> to do in response to suffering. If there's any positive action you can take, find the courage or the way—and do it. If there's nothing you can do externally, concentrate on your inner response. Pray for consolation and hope; be open to the mysteries of your heart's healing.

10.

Pain and tragedy can result from a world that is still unfinished and evolving. In the beginning, God started to draw order out of chaos, but pockets of chaos remain. Have patience with the incompleteness of the world and its creatures, including yourself.

11.

God invites us to join the Divine plan to ultimately conquer sin and chaos and move the world to completion and peace. Accept God's offer of partnership and use your creative efforts to end suffering.

ELF
HILL
SHELTER

12.

Good people everywhere are working hard to build a better world and to free it of suffering. Link arms with them and share their goals.

13.

Sometimes suffering comes into your life because of your own decisions and actions. Determine how you may be contributing to your suffering and what you can do to create healing.

14.

God doesn't interfere with human freedom, even when that freedom allows persons to make choices that are destructive to themselves and others. Respect the power of your free choice and use it for good.

15.

Sunlight is the best disinfectant.
Place yourself in the warm
radiance of God's healing care
and unconditional love.

16.

When deep suffering or loss
befalls you, it will take time to
be set free of your trauma or
broken heart. Remember that
through it all, God's healing
love is at work.

17.

Let your pain and uncertainty move you naturally toward prayer. A rich prayer life can be an unexpected positive that results from the negative of suffering.

18.

Crying, screaming, and raging can be prayers. Life has dealt you a cruel blow. Name your hurt to God.

19.

When you find it hard to pray, surrender to the emptiness. God is close to the brokenhearted.

20.

God isn't hiding along the pathway of life ready to ambush you and punish you for your failings and shortcomings. Remove any traces of "ambush theology" that you may harbor.

21.

Suffering can confer a coldness
on your life. When it does,
warm yourself with nature,
music, art, humor, laughter.

22.

In your sorrow, look for new
awakenings and rebirth—and
the dawn beyond the darkness.
Like a sunflower, keep turning
to the Light and you'll find
hope, despite the passing clouds.

23.

Trust that, in the midst of what doesn't seem to make sense, God has only loving plans for you. Give yourself over completely to God's love.

24.

Good parents care for a sick child until healing comes. If it doesn't, they stand by lovingly until the child passes to new life. Know that your Divine Parent is even more eager to bring you to wholeness.

25.

In suffering, you can discover
there are circumstances over
which you have no control.
Accept your own finiteness
as you rest in the Infinite.

26.

You may not be free to avoid suffering, but you're always free to shape your attitude toward suffering. Use your freedom to choose courageously and wisely.

27.

Allow suffering to enhance your humanity. When you trustingly bear some deep sorrow, your heart grows in wisdom and grace.

28.

As you lean into your suffering,
you are linked in spirit with
suffering people of every place
and age. United with them, let
your compassion come to life—
in prayer, words, and actions
that help those who suffer.

29.

You can make sense out of suffering by embracing God who draws meaning from it through your own loving response. Know that the God who brought order out of chaos can create something noble from your confusion and tears.

30.

With healing, bones become
stronger in the places that
were broken. The same is true
of broken hearts. Open yourself
to the healing energy embedded
deep in the universe and in
God's heart.

31.

Just as the strokes of a surgeon's knife can bring about immense good—even the saving of a life—so can God create good out of apparent evil. Trust in the healing hand of God, who is wiser than any doctor.

32.

Suffering can be purifying. Let your suffering help you to place life's petty annoyances in perspective and to point you to what's truly important.

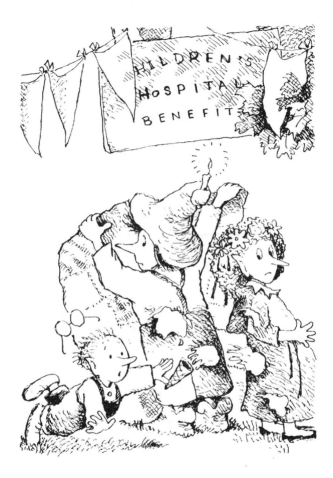

33.

Suffering can be transformative.
Let your suffering open you to
a deeper capacity for loving, to
cherishing the persons who
enrich your life.

34.

Embrace suffering as a natural part of life. Just as shadow and light define each other and one cannot exist without the other, so it is with suffering and joy. You can't know real joy if you've never known real suffering.

IN
MEMORY
OF
MOM

35.

You can't choose not to suffer, for we'll all surely suffer. But you can choose not to let suffering make you embittered, withdrawn, paranoid, or hostile. The question is not "How can I avoid suffering in my life?" but "How can this suffering make my life more alive?"

36.

In the midst of suffering, trust that either your burden will lighten or you'll receive the strength to endure. The way to get beyond suffering is to go through it—with your hand in God's.

Jack Wintz is a Franciscan priest, a writer, and an editor with St. Anthony Messenger Press in Cincinnati, Ohio. He is the author of the book *Lights: Revelations of God's Goodness*.

Illustrator for the Abbey Press Elf-help Books, **R.W. Alley** also illustrates and writes children's books. He lives in Barrington, Rhode Island, with his wife, daughter, and son.

The Story of the Abbey Press Elves

The engaging figures that populate the Abbey Press "elf-help" line of publications and products first appeared in 1987 on the pages of a small self-help book called *Be-good-to-yourself Therapy*. Shaped by the publishing staff's vision and defined in R.W. Alley's inventive illustrations, they lived out author Cherry Hartman's gentle, self-nurturing advice with charm, poignancy, and humor.

Reader response was so enthusiastic that more Elf-help Books were soon under way, a still-growing series that has inspired a line of related gift products.

The especially endearing character featured in the early books—sporting a cap with a mood-changing candle in its peak—has since been joined by a spirited female elf with flowers in her hair.

These two exuberant, sensitive, resourceful, kindhearted, lovable sprites, along with their lively elfin community, reveal what's truly important as they offer messages of joy and wonder, playfulness and co-creation, wholeness and serenity, the miracle of life and the mystery of God's love.

With wisdom and whimsy, these little creatures with long noses demonstrate the elf-help way to a rich and fulfilling life.

Elf-help Books

...adding "a little character" and a lot
of help to self-help reading!

Gratitude Therapy	#20105
Trust-in-God Therapy	#20119
Elf-help for Overcoming Depression	#20134
New Baby Therapy	#20140
Teacher Therapy	#20145
Stress Therapy	#20153
Making-sense-out-of-suffering Therapy	#20156
Get Well Therapy	#20157
Anger Therapy	#20127
Caregiver Therapy	#20164
Self-esteem Therapy	#20165
Peace Therapy	#20176
Friendship Therapy	#20174
Christmas Therapy (color edition) $5.95	#20175
Happy Birthday Therapy	#20181
Forgiveness Therapy	#20184
Keep-life-simple Therapy	#20185
Celebrate-your-womanhood Therapy	#20189
Acceptance Therapy (color edition) $5.95	#20182

Book price is $4.95 unless otherwise noted.
Available at your favorite giftshop or bookstore—
or directly from One Caring Place, Abbey Press
Publications, St. Meinrad, IN 47577.
Or call 1-800-325-2511.
www.carenotes.com